OLD AND YOUNG

Tom Hughes

 Enslow Publishing
101 W. 23rd Street
Suite 240
New York, NY 10011
USA
enslow.com

Published in 2017 by Enslow Publishing, LLC
101 W. 23rd Street, Suite 240, New York, NY 10011

Library of Congress Cataloging-in-Publication Data
Names: Hughes, Tom, 1980– author.
Title: Old and young / Tom Hughes.
Description: New York, NY, USA : Enslow Publishing, LLC, [2017] | Series: All about opposites |
Audience: Ages 5 up. | Audience: Pre-school, excluding K. | Includes bibliographical references and index.
Identifiers: LCCN 2016022720 | ISBN 9780766081154 (library bound) | ISBN 9780766081116 (pbk.) |
ISBN 9780766081147 (6-pack)
Subjects: LCSH: Older people—Juvenile literature. | Aging—Juvenile literature. | Youth—Juvenile
literature.=Classification: LCC HQ1061 .H823 2017 | DDC 305.26—dc23
LC record available at https://lccn.loc.gov/2016022720

Printed in China

To Our Readers: We have done our best to make sure all websites in this book were active and appropriate when we went to press. However, the author and the publisher have no control over and assume no liability for the material available on those websites or on any websites they may link to. Any comments or suggestions can be sent by e-mail to customerservice@enslow.com.

Photo Credits: Cover, p. 1 (top) StudioPortoSabbia/Shutterstock.com; cover, p. 1 (bottom) Mikkel Bigandt/Shutterstock.com; pp. 3 (left), 12 Dafinka/Shutterstock.com; pp. 3 (center), 9 AnetaPics/iStock/Thinkstock; pp. 3 (right), 14 Gennady Stetsenko/Shutterstock.com; pp. 4-5 Tom Wang/Shutterstock.com; p. 6 TACstock/Shutterstock.com; p. 7 pavla/Shutterstock.com; p. 8 studioportosabbia/iStock/Thinkstock; p. 10 sjallenphotography/iStock/Thinkstock p. 11 MaraZe/Shutterstock.com; p. 13 Paulbr/iStock/Thinkstock; p. 15 Everything/Shutterstock.com; p. 16 Koldunov Alexey/Shutterstock.com; p. 17 fiphoto/Shutterstock.com; p. 18 © iStockphoto.com/ratmaner; p. 19 Nitr/Shutterstock.com; pp. 20-21 Yuri Arcurs/E+/Getty Images; p. 22 bikeriderlondon/Shutterstock.com.

Contents

Words to Know 3

Old and Young 4

Read More 24

Websites 24

Index 24

Words to Know

building

puppy

tree

Old and young
are opposites.

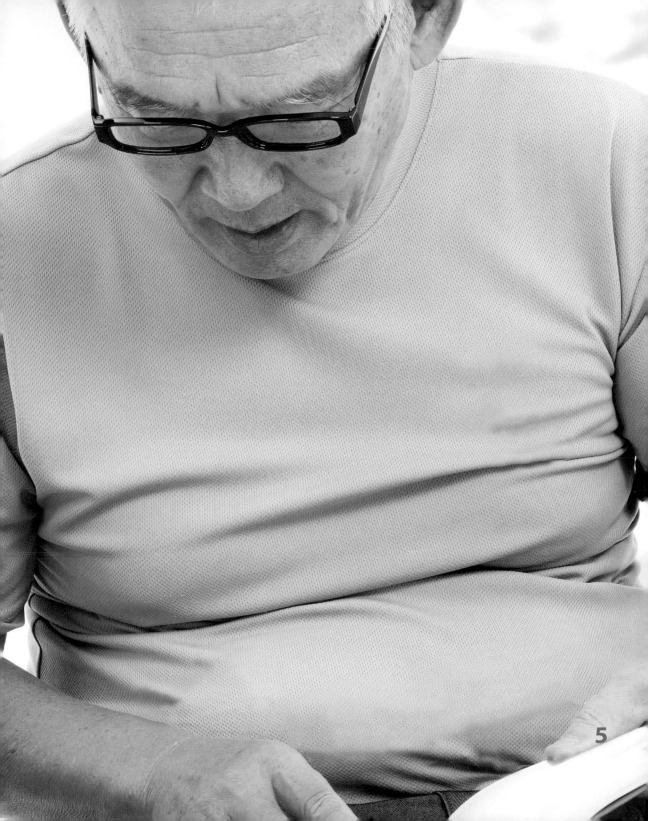

A grandparent is old.

A baby is young.

This dog is old.

A puppy is young.

This cat is old.

A kitten is young.

Some buildings are old.

Some buildings are new.

Some trees are old.

Some trees are young.

Clothes can get old.

Or clothes can be new.

Even food can get old.

Fresh food is best.

Young comes before old.

Old comes after young.

Old and young people can have fun together!

Read More

Hills, Tad. *What's Up, Duck: A Book of Opposites*. New York, NY: Schwartz & Wade, 2008.

Horacek, Petr. *Animal Opposites*. Somerville, MA: Candlewick Press, 2013.

Websites

A Game of Opposites
www.meddybemps.com/opposites/Index.html
See if you can match the opposites!

Sesame Street
www.sesamestreet.org/videos?video=9fec40f2-156a-11dd-bb51-597ab51d2e81
Learn more about opposites.

Index

baby, 7

buildings, 12–13

cat, 10

clothes, 16–17

dog, 8

food, 18–19

grandparent, 6

kitten, 11

puppy, 9

trees, 14–15

Guided Reading Level: B
Guided Reading Leveling System is based on the guidelines recommended by Fountas and Pinnell.

Word Count: 79